Francis Frith's

The Cinque Ports
and the Two Ancient Towns

Photographic Memories

Francis Frith's
The Cinque Ports
and the Two Ancient Towns

Alan Kay

First published in the United Kingdom in 2002 by
Frith Book Company Ltd

Hardback Edition
1-85937-492-1

British Library Cataloguing in Publication Data

Francis Frith's The Cinque Ports and the Two Ancient Towns
Alan Kay

Frith Book Company Ltd
Frith's Barn, Teffont,
Salisbury, Wiltshire SP3 5QP
Tel: +44 (0) 1722 716 376
Email: info@francisfrith.co.uk
www.francisfrith.co.uk

Printed and bound in Great Britain

Front Cover: Dover, The Promenade 1924 76042

Contents

Francis Frith: *Victorian Pioneer*

FRANCIS FRITH, Victorian founder of the world-famous photographic archive, was a complex and multi-talented man. A devout Quaker and a highly successful Victorian businessman, he was both philosophic by nature and pioneering in outlook.

By 1855 Francis Frith had already established a wholesale grocery business in Liverpool, and sold it for the astonishing sum of £200,000, which is the equivalent today of over £15,000,000. Now a multi-millionaire, he was able to indulge his passion for travel. As a child he had pored over travel books written by early explorers, and his fancy and imagination had been stirred by family holidays to the sublime mountain regions of Wales and Scotland. 'What a land of spirit-stirring and enriching scenes and places!' he had written. He was to return to these scenes of grandeur in later years to 'recapture the thousands of vivid and tender memories', but with a different purpose. Now in his thirties, and captivated by the new science of photography, Frith set out on a series of pioneering journeys to the Nile regions that occupied him from 1856 until 1860.

Intrigue and Adventure

He took with him on his travels a specially-designed wicker carriage that acted as both dark-room and sleeping chamber. These far-flung journeys were packed with intrigue and adventure. In his life story, written when he was sixty-three, Frith tells of being held captive by bandits, and of fighting 'an awful midnight battle to the very point of surrender with a deadly pack of hungry, wild dogs'. Sporting flowing Arab costume, Frith arrived at Akaba by camel seventy years before Lawrence, where he encountered 'desert princes and rival sheikhs, blazing with jewel-hilted swords'.

During these extraordinary adventures he was assiduously exploring the desert regions bordering the Nile and patiently recording the antiquities and peoples with his camera. He was the first photographer to venture beyond the sixth cataract. Africa was still the mysterious 'Dark Continent', and Stanley and Livingstone's historic meeting was a decade into the future. The conditions for picture taking confound belief. He laboured for hours in his wicker dark-room in the sweltering heat of the desert, while the volatile chemicals fizzed dangerously in their trays. Often he was forced to work in remote tombs and caves where conditions were cooler. Back in London he exhibited his photographs and was 'rapturously cheered' by members of the Royal Society. His reputation as a photographer was made overnight. An eminent modern historian has likened their impact on the population of the time to that on our own generation of the first photographs taken on the surface of the moon.

Venture of a Life-Time

Characteristically, Frith quickly spotted the opportunity to create a new business as a specialist publisher of photographs. He lived in an era of immense and sometimes violent change. For the poor in the early part of Victoria's reign work was a drudge and the hours long, and people had precious little free time to enjoy themselves. Most had no transport other than a cart or gig at their disposal, and had not travelled far beyond the boundaries of their own town or village. However,

by the 1870s, the railways had threaded their way across the country, and Bank Holidays and half-day Saturdays had been made obligatory by Act of Parliament. All of a sudden the ordinary working man and his family were able to enjoy days out and see a little more of the world.

With characteristic business acumen, Francis Frith foresaw that these new tourists would enjoy having souvenirs to commemorate their days out. In 1860 he married Mary Ann Rosling and set out with the intention of photographing every city, town and village in Britain. For the next thirty years he travelled the country by train and by pony and trap, producing fine photographs of seaside resorts and beauty spots that were keenly bought by millions of Victorians. These prints were painstakingly pasted into family albums and pored over during the dark nights of winter, rekindling precious memories of summer excursions.

The Rise of Frith & Co

Frith's studio was soon supplying retail shops all over the country. To meet the demand he gathered about him a small team of photographers, and published the work of independent artist-photographers of the calibre of Roger Fenton and Francis Bedford. In order to gain some understanding of the scale of Frith's business one only has to look at the catalogue issued by Frith & Co in 1886: it runs to some 670 pages, listing not only many thousands of views of the British Isles but also many photographs of most European countries, and China, Japan, the USA and Canada – note the sample page shown above from the hand-written *Frith & Co* ledgers detailing pictures taken. By 1890 Frith had created the greatest specialist photographic publishing company in the world,

Frith's death, a new card measuring 5.5 x 3.5 inches became the standard format, but it was not until 1902 that the divided back came into being, with address and message on one face and a full-size illustration on the other. *Frith & Co* were in the vanguard of postcard development, and Frith's sons Eustace and Cyril continued their father's monumental task, expanding the number of views offered to the public and recording more and more places in Britain, as the coasts and countryside were opened up to mass travel.

Francis Frith died in 1898 at his villa in Cannes, his great project still growing. The archive he created continued in business for another seventy years. By 1970 it contained over a third of a million pictures of 7,000 cities, towns and villages. The massive photographic record Frith has left to us stands as a living monument to a special and very remarkable man.

with over 2,000 outlets – more than the combined number that Boots and WH Smith have today! The picture on the right shows the *Frith & Co* display board at Ingleton in the Yorkshire Dales. Beautifully constructed with mahogany frame and gilt inserts, it could display up to a dozen local scenes.

Postcard Bonanza

The ever-popular holiday postcard we know today took many years to develop. In 1870 the Post Office issued the first plain cards, with a pre-printed stamp on one face. In 1894 they allowed other publishers' cards to be sent through the mail with an attached adhesive halfpenny stamp. Demand grew rapidly, and in 1895 a new size of postcard was permitted called the court card, but there was little room for illustration. In 1899, a year after

Frith's Archive: *A Unique Legacy*

FRANCIS FRITH'S legacy to us today is of immense significance and value, for the magnificent archive of evocative photographs he created provides a unique record of change in 7,000 cities, towns and villages throughout Britain over a century and more. Frith and his fellow studio photographers revisited locations many times down the years to update their views, compiling for us an enthralling and colourful pageant of British life and character.

We tend to think of Frith's sepia views of Britain as nostalgic, for most of us use them to conjure up memories of places in our own lives with which we have family associations. It often makes us forget that to Francis Frith they were records of daily life as it was actually being lived in the cities, towns and villages of his day. The Victorian age was one of great and often bewildering change for ordinary people, and though the pictures evoke an impression of slower times, life was as busy and hectic as it is today.

We are fortunate that Frith was a photographer of the people, dedicated to recording the minutiae of everyday life. For it is this sheer wealth of visual data, the painstaking chronicle of changes in dress, transport, street layouts, buildings, housing, engineering and landscape that captivates us so much today. His remarkable images offer us a powerful link with the past and with the lives of our ancestors.

Today's Technology

Computers have now made it possible for Frith's many thousands of images to be accessed almost instantly. In the Frith archive today, each photograph is carefully 'digitised' then stored on a CD Rom. Frith archivists can locate a single photograph amongst thousands within seconds. Views can be catalogued and sorted under a variety of categories of place and content to the immediate benefit of researchers.

Inexpensive reference prints can be created for them at the touch of a mouse button, and a wide range of books and other printed materials assembled and published for a wider, more general readership - in the next twelve months over a hundred Frith local history titles will be published! The day-to-day workings of the archive are very different from how they were in Francis Frith's time: imagine the herculean task of sorting through eleven tons of glass negatives as Frith had to do to locate a particular sequence of pictures! Yet

See Frith at www.francisfrith.co.uk

the archive still prides itself on maintaining the same high standards of excellence laid down by Francis Frith, including the painstaking cataloguing and indexing of every view.

It is curious to reflect on how the internet now allows researchers in America and elsewhere greater instant access to the archive than Frith himself ever enjoyed. Many thousands of individual views can be called up on screen within seconds on one of the Frith internet sites, enabling people living continents away to revisit the streets of their ancestral home town, or view places in Britain where they have enjoyed holidays. Many overseas researchers welcome the chance to view special theme selections, such as transport, sports, costume and ancient monuments.

We are certain that Francis Frith would have heartily approved of these modern developments in imaging techniques, for he himself was always working at the very limits of Victorian photographic technology.

The Value of the Archive Today

Because of the benefits brought by the computer, Frith's images are increasingly studied by social historians, by researchers into genealogy and ancestory, by architects, town planners, and by teachers and schoolchildren involved in local history projects.

In addition, the archive offers every one of us an opportunity to examine the places where we and our families have lived and worked down the years. Highly successful in Frith's own era, the archive is now, a century and more on, entering a new phase of popularity.

The Past in Tune with the Future

Historians consider the Francis Frith Collection to be of prime national importance. It is the only archive of its kind remaining in private ownership and has been valued at a million pounds. However, this figure is now rapidly increasing as digital technology enables more and more people around the world to enjoy its benefits.

Francis Frith's archive is now housed in an historic timber barn in the beautiful village of Teffont in Wiltshire. Its founder would not recognize the archive office as it is today. In place of the many thousands of dusty boxes containing glass plate negatives and an all-pervading odour of photographic chemicals, there are now ranks of computer screens. He would be amazed to watch his images travelling round the world at unimaginable speeds through network and internet lines.

The archive's future is both bright and exciting. Francis Frith, with his unshakeable belief in making photographs available to the greatest number of people, would undoubtedly approve of what is being done today with his lifetime's work. His photographs, depicting our shared past, are now bringing pleasure and enlightenment to millions around the world a century and more after his death.

The Cinque Ports - *An Introduction*

THERE has always been a certain aura of romance about the Cinque Ports of Kent and Sussex. These ports were of supreme importance to England in the 11th and 12th centuries as the main line of defence against foreign invaders. Many people believe 'cinque' to mean five: thus confusion occurs when they find that the Confederation consisted of seven towns, and it is even more confusing to find that there were at least 25 towns connected in some form or another. More confusion occurs when they find that the word is always pronounced in its ancient form, 'sink', and not in the French way, 'sank'.

This volume on the Confederation of the Cinque Ports links photographs from the Frith archive, which show the ports as they were some fifty to one hundred years ago, with text describing their importance some six to ten centuries earlier.

The Cinque Ports Confederation of ports goes back to 1050, when Edward the Confessor traded

Above: **Sandwich**
The Danish Viking Ship at Pegwell Bay c1955 S60023
This replica of a Danish Viking ship still stands at Pegwell Bay, near Sandwich

Left: **Hastings**
The Castle Ruins 1894 34434
Hastings was possibly the first of the Cinque Ports, providing 21 ships out of the original 57. Its importance was recognised by the Romans during their occupation, and it was important in Saxon times. A castle built later now lies in ruins on the cliff top.

many privileges in return for the use of ships and men to repel the many raiders who came to pillage and burn. The original five ports were all recorded in the Domesday Book. For centuries our south-east coastline had been attacked by Romans, Saxons, Vikings (see No S60023) and Normans, and local seamen were called upon to defend their towns.

England's legendary maritime power had its beginnings centuries ago, and has played an unrivalled part in the development of our country. The establishment of the Cinque Ports was undoubtedly instrumental in the founding of what was later to become our Royal Navy. The initial importance of the Cinque Ports lay in their situation: they face the continent at the point where the English Channel is at its narrowest. King John realised he badly needed some form of defence to control these narrow seas against invaders from France or Flanders, and the Cinque Ports are thus the second oldest institution in our country, outside the monarchy. King John also realised that an alliance of our best sailors and fighting men under his command could also be of great value in maintaining his often tenuous grip on the throne.

No permanent solution to the defence of our country was discovered until the mercenary system of buying off invaders was abandoned and replaced by 'ship service', the provision of ships and fighting men in return for a considerable degree of self-government. The original five ports all had harbours and possessed seaworthy fishing fleets, manned by skilful crews who built their own boats. At this time there was no such thing as a passenger ship, a cargo ship, or a warship - the same vessel at different times might be all three.

It is fortunate that details of ship service are recorded in the Domesday Book, which was completed in 1086. Within the next one hundred and fifty years, the barons of the Cinque Ports supplied 57 ships, each fully crewed with 21 men and a boy to fight on behalf of the Crown, and also to ferry officers of the state across the Channel. When not fighting against invaders, the Portsmen were fishermen and pirates. They also became well-nigh ungovernable, and were in constant conflict with the Crown. They gained a reputation as the most infamous pirates of all, often slow to observe any national peace treaties or truces. Effective action to restrain their violence and their piracy, wrecking and robbery on the high seas proved almost impossible. The various monarchs often needed the service of the Cinque Ports more than the seamen needed the state.

As early as 1202, the ships of the Cinque Ports were at sea in force against the French attacks: a large fleet defeated the French, and 200 ships were captured by the Cinque Portsmen. This was the first of many subsequent battles. Earlier, the Straits of

Hythe, The Quay c1955 H141005
Hythe never reached the power and prosperity of Dover or Hastings, and only supplied 5 ships and 100 men for the King's use. The port later lost its harbour to the vagaries of sea and weather, and the town is now separated from the seas by a great expanse of shingle.

Dover had been an Anglo-Norman sea, a bridge between two countries sharing the same Royal house. However, when Normandy was lost to the English crown in 1206, the Channel and the Straits of Dover became a no-man's-land, a battlefield between two unfriendly powers. The 13th century thus became known as 'the violent century in the narrow sea'.

It was not until 1260 that the King first granted a Charter to the Confederation of the Cinque Ports (earlier charters had been granted to the ports individually). As part of the contract, the ports were to supply to the King 57 ships fully manned for 15 days in return for substantial privileges. If the 15 days were exceeded, the Charters provided a specified payment of 6d a day for the Master, 3d a day for the rest of the crew, and 1d a day for the boy! 15 days would not allow for any long voyages, but that was not what the King wanted. He just wanted ships to repulse raids in a short and sharp clash, or to ferry him, his men and goods across to France as the need arose. Local knowledge of the Straits of

Dover proved invaluable.

For this service to the Crown the ports were given many privileges, and were independent of the counties in which they lay. They were not subject to direct taxation, being free of all tolls and customs duties, and they were free to trade unhindered by any merchant monopoly. They also had the right to seize unclaimed or stolen goods, and the 'right of wreck' as well. This stated that any vessel, goods or fish washed ashore must be offered to the Lord Warden of the Cinque Ports. A beached whale was thus offered to the Queen Mother, as Lord Warden, a few years ago, but was tactfully declined.

The Ports could also erect pillories, and could imprison and execute thieves and murderers without trial. Barbaric punishments were common. Dover was often the preferred port when the death penalty was imposed: there, the criminals were flung over the Shakespeare Cliff to experience a speedy death from broken limbs, whereas at Hastings and Sandwich they were tied to stakes and left to the rising tide. The Ports were also granted

New Romney High Street c1955
N141004
New Romney is only called 'New' to distinguish it from the ancient Cinque Port of Old Romney, the original port whose silting up left the present town some two miles from the sea. The port supplied 5 ships to the Confederation.

the right to land their fish at the great fish market of Great Yarmouth. The problem for Cinque Port fishermen was to land their catch and get it to market before it became so bad as to be unsaleable. Hence their right to sell at the Herring Fairs at Yarmouth, before returning to Kent, was extremely valuable. From all these privileges the Cinque Port towns grew rich and powerful.

The heyday of the Cinque Ports lasted for less than two centuries, and it fell into decline around 1380 due to the King's growing powers in national government; increasingly, he was becoming unwilling to brook any independent action from any group of towns. Also, once a permanent navy was created, vessels became larger, and harbours became deeper; there was thus a shift of influence to Portsmouth, Plymouth and other larger ports to the west.

Another reason for the decline of the Cinque Ports was the silting up of their harbours through the changes which the coastline of Kent and Sussex underwent in the Middle Ages. The sea built up bars of shingle and sand, so that Sandwich is now two

miles from the sea, Romney is high and dry, and Hythe is a mile inland. Today Dover is the only one of the original harbours which has retained its importance.

Action against the Spanish Armada in 1588 was the last recorded naval engagement in which the Cinque Ports participated: at a cost of £33,000 they fitted out and crewed six galleons and supplied five fire ships, which did much damage to the Spanish fleet.

Although the influence of the Ports declined over the centuries, the Confederation still survives, if only for ceremonial purposes. The Barons of the Cinque Ports still attend the Coronation service by right, and previously had the honour of carrying the canopy over the monarch and to dine at the Coronation banquet. The last time this occurred was at the coronation of King Edward VII in 1910. The Court of Shepway still meets annually under the Lord Warden (which is said to be the oldest English office), and the Courts of Brotherhood and Guestling still meet with appropriate ceremony to discuss the business of the Ports.

Sandwich, The Barbican c1955 S60018
Sandwich was another Cinque Port which later silted up and fell into decline. As a Channel port, it had a long and violent history as a target for French and Danish raids. The Barbican Gate was built in 1539 as a main entrance to the town.

Dover, The Castle Walls c1955 D50017
Dover also supplied 21 ships for the defence of the country. The fortifications shown here have been used and added to during every phase of our turbulent past from Roman times to World War II.

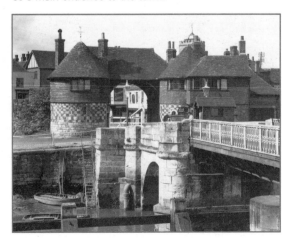

Hastings

THE five Head Cinque Ports were selected as being conveniently spaced along the most critical section of the Kent and Sussex coastline. They were equals, though much has been written to prove or disprove the superiority of one port over another. The fact that Hastings is or was always named first in the list probably means no more than that it comes first reading from west to east in a geographical order, although the fact that there is one complete lion on its coast of arms against half lions on the others is said to indicate its status as the chief port of the Confederation. This is naturally disputed by historians of the other towns.

The Battle of Hastings in 1066 between the Norman and Saxon armies (the date remembered by most schoolchildren) did not take place here, but on a hill some seven miles inland. William the Conqueror was able to land relatively unopposed, as the Cinque Ports fleet was supporting King Harold off our north-east coast repelling other forces from Norway. Later, William realised that he needed the Portsmen more than they needed him, and confirmed the pre-Conquest agreements with the Cinque Ports. These ports were of crucial importance to him in securing the Dover Straits. The original port of Hastings was possibly the premier port until the Great Storm ruined its first harbour, and in 1069 seamen from Hastings drove off a strong Danish raiding fleet.

Hastings, The Beach c1955 H36020
In the Old Town is the Stade, a fishermen's beach cluttered with fishing boats, tackle and outbuildings. With no natural harbour since the 13th century, fishing boats have always been hauled up the shingle beach, as we see here and in picture no H36022.

▼ **Hastings, The Cliffs 1894** 34439

▼ **Hastings, The Beach c1955** H36022

▲ **Hastings, The Castle 1890** 22792
The first castle here was a wooden castle erected by William the Conqueror around 1066, the earthworks of which are shown on the Bayeux Tapestry. Much of the Norman castle was destroyed by landslips in the 13th century. The ruins which now remain are part of the curtain wall. Outside the fragmented walls is a honeycomb of passages, dungeons and storehouses.

Hastings, The Dolphin c1955 H36019
A unique feature of Hastings Old Town is the cluster of tarred wood fishermen's hutments or net shops. They were built for drying fishing nets and storing equipment. There are still over 40 of these tall, thin, weather-boarded gable-roofed net shops, but there were over 100 of them at the beginning of the 20th century.

The Old Town is all that remains of the fishing village, now occupied by the centre of the present town. Earlier, the little Saxon town of 'Hasteg' with its harbour was granted by Canute to the monastery of Fecamp in Normandy. In 1148, crews from the Cinque Port helped to take Lisbon, and a priest from Hastings became Bishop of Lisbon. Silting affected the harbour in the 12th century, and the silting was accentuated by the Great Storm in the 13th century. The original town declined, and what is now called the Old Town started to develop.

After the middle of the 16th century unsuccessful efforts were made to build a new harbour, but the early harbour works were largely destroyed in the heavy storms of 1597. From being one of the most powerful of the Cinque Ports, Hastings now fell into decay.

► **Hastings, The Old Town c1955** H36016
Hastings is a complex town of three distinct parts: the Old Town, with its ruined castle; St Leonards farther west, founded as a fashionable resort in the 1820s; and the Victorian and modern central area between. As we can see here, Hastings, like Dover, another Cinque Port, is dominated by its castle on Castle Hill.

◄ **Hastings, The View from the Pier 1925**
77971
The social class-consciousness of Victorian times gave Hastings a status above the day-tripper resorts of Margate, Southend or Brighton. By the mid 19th century, the town had expanded to take in St Leonards to the west and a fairly serious fishing industry in the Old Town to the east.

Hastings, The Promenade c1955 H36044

Hastings, The View from the Pier 1925 77974

◀ **Hastings, The Edinburgh Hotel c1955** H36048
The decline of Hastings' importance was halted: Hastings was reborn at the end of the 18th century, when the first seaside visitors started to arrive about 1770. Like so many southern resorts, Hastings owed its beginnings to an 18th-century medical man, a certain Dr Ballie, who advocated salt-water bathing as a panacea for many ailments. The Victorian hotel architecture we see here and in No 77974 developed from the earlier lodging houses and boarding houses.

**Hastings
The Esplanade 1925**
77977

Hastings, The Promenade c1955 H36027

▲ Above: **Hastings, The Beach 1925** 77982

▶ **Hastings, The Bandstand 1925** 77987
This scene of the bandstand on the sea front gives us a nostalgic memory of seaside entertainments in the early 20th century. Regimental bands would undertake summer tours of the resorts on the south coast, where it seems more visitors enjoyed the music free of charge rather than pay for seats.

Hythe

HYTHE means 'a haven or hythe of the estuary'; Hythe provided 5 ships and a 100 men for the King's use in return for Cinque Port privileges. Its earliest charter is dated 1278, but by 1450 its harbour facilities were abandoned owing to the constant deposition of silt. The old harbour, of which there is no trace today, was a harbour of great importance; it was the central Cinque Port geographically between Sandwich and Dover to the east, and Hastings and Rye to the west.

Originally a river flowed eastwards over the present Romney Marsh, reaching the Channel around the site of present-day Hythe. By Saxon times the river turned south to a harbour near Romney itself, but part of the old estuary remained; this was usable for a time as a harbour for Hythe. Hythe then developed alongside the estuary to become the very long stretched-out town.

Hythe flourished for some 150 years during the Cinque Ports era, but in the 14th century the harbour finally silted up and the port fell into decline. The deposition of harbour silt added to the other disasters of the century. A great fire in 1400 destroyed some 200 houses – there had also been damage from raids by the French. Between 1337

Hythe, General View 1903 50374

and 1350 the French were in the ascendant, and raided all the Cinque Ports; in 1339 the French attacks destroyed every ship in Hythe. Hythe also suffered from the Great Plague and winter storms. The King actually excused the town from ship service for a period, so that the town might recover. By the time of the Spanish Armada, Hythe could no longer meet its obligations to the Confederation.

Another era opened in Napoleonic times when the Royal Military Canal was dug; it ran roughly along the line of the original estuary, partly as a moat against the feared French invasion.

Hythe, High and Dry c1960 H141060

Hythe, The Quay c1955 H141008
The sea which had so devastated old Winchelsea had the opposite effect at Hythe, where the old harbour was starting to silt up around 1230. As the tidal scour increased, the shingle was carried eastwards to mass at Hythe, and thus it smothered the entrance to the original Hythe Haven.

Hythe, The Canal 1899 44787

Hythe, The Canal Bridge 1903 50378
The Royal Military Canal, shaded by tall trees as it runs through the heart of the town, was constructed in 1804 as part of the anti-invasion defences against Napoleon. The Canal runs 23 miles from Hythe to the Rother, and was so constructed that artillery could be placed to cover every yard of it. By the end of the 19th century ,the canal was used for the transport of coal and other heavy goods by barge between Hythe and Rye.

Hythe, The Beach c1960 H141059

Hythe, The Beach c1960 H141074
By Georgian times, Hythe had settled to a position as a Kent market village half a mile from the shingle beaches of the Channel coast. Visitors to a small seaside community came to the areas of Hythe nearer the sea.

◄ **Hythe
The Beach
c1950**
H141302

◄ **Hythe**
The Promenade c1960
H141058

▼ **Hythe, The Hotel Imperial 1902** 48827
In Victorian times, the Hotel Imperial, facing
the beach, catered for the more affluent
type of visitor.

◄ **Hythe**
The Boat Stage
the Royal Military
Canal c1950 H141301
Every two years ,Hythe
stages its waterborne
Venetian Fair on the
Royal Military Canal, a
summer carnival
attraction visited by
tourists from afar.

▼ **Hythe, The Hill c1955** H141013
Near the top of the hill stands St Leonard's church, built around 1100, one of four which existed before the town's decline. It is often described as a 'herring church', built when the Cinque Ports enjoyed prosperity from the herring harvest from the sea. The tower was destroyed by the earth tremors of 1739, and was rebuilt in 1750. The crypt contains some 4000 human remains and skulls whose real origins are unknown, carefully arranged on shelves.

▼ **Hythe, The Wesleyan Church 1899** 44789

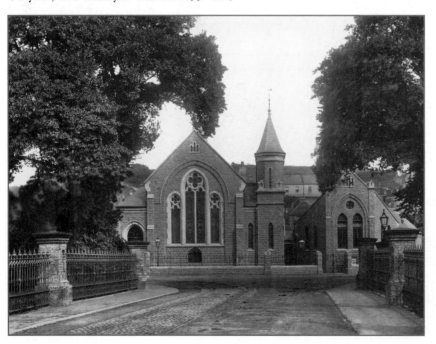

▲ **Hythe, Main Street c1950** H141312
The busy main street of Hythe is the lowest of a succession of parallel terraces rising from the canal to the parish church. The old quays of the original Cinque Port were probably behind the present shops to the left. Motor traffic often has difficulty in squeezing through the narrow street, which was not built for modern traffic conditions.

◄ **Hythe
Main Street
c1950**
H141311

**Hythe, High Street
c1950** H141318
The present High Street
is long and narrow with
a gentle curve. On the
left is the old Town Hall
of 1794 with its open-
columned ground
storey. From this
section of the High
Street steep lanes and
narrow alleys lead up to
the terraced streets on
the slope above.

◄ **Hythe
Main Street
c1950** H141314

Hythe, The Miniature Railway c1960 H141042
The railway's usual name is the Romney, Hythe and Dymchurch Railway; it opened in 1927 to link up the main railway termini at Hythe and New Romney, and a five-mile extension to Dymchurch opened in 1929. Though the gauge is only 15 inches, the railway is a great attraction to tourists, and it is also used as a 'school bus', conveying some 250 children daily from Hythe to New Romney.

▼ **Hythe, The Institute 1899** 44790

Hythe, The Grove 1902 48829
The Grove is a couple of miles west of Hythe; it was the early site of Shepway Cross, where the Court of Shepway met to carry out the official business of the Cinque Ports. This Court was the link between the Confederation and the central government. The name derives from Shipway, and thus must originate from a time before the sea channel silted up. The name is continued to the present day: the local government authority is Shepway District Council.

New Romney, High Street c1955 N141011

The long, wide High Street is wide enough to aid New Romney's development as a market for the Marsh. The long, straight, country town High Street has a grey-painted Town Hall on the south side. On the right is the red brick Priory House, which still has Dickensian shop windows on either side of the portico. Many buildings are half-timbered, and some have floor levels a few feet below the present High Street.

New Romney, High Street c1955 N141004

New Romney

THERE was once a single port at Romney called Rummenea by the Saxons, but a vast upheaval in the 13th century changed the low-lying coastline of Kent from Romney to Thanet. The eastward drift of shingle and sand from Dungeness to the Thames Estuary left Old Romney over two miles from the sea, and thus its wharf was unusable. As the sea retreated, the change in the course of the Rother made Winchelsea and Rye into islands, and New Romney developed nearer the sea. Old Romney and New Romney were differentiated as two communities by the early 13th century.

Records of New Romney show that the town was a small port in about 1100; however, like other harbours on the marshes, it quickly silted up. Much of what is now Romney Marsh was once tidal water, but by the time of the end of the Cinque Ports' importance, New Romney was surrounded by choked-up creeks, with the sea over a mile away.

Traditionally, New Romney is at the centre of the Cinque Port Confederation, having Hastings, Rye and Winchelsea to the west, and Hythe, Dover and Sandwich to the east. Thanks to this central position, it became the meeting place of the Brotherhood and the venue for the Portsmen's own court. In the early days of the Cinque Ports, Romney had to furnish 5 ships, each manned with a boy, for the King's Ship Service, but by the Siege of Calais in 1347 it only supplied 4 ships. The English fleet was some 700 ships strong at the Siege of Calais, but fewer than a quarter of them came from the Cinque Ports. Romney suffered from many raids by the French, and often raided France in return. In 1337 French raids destroyed every single ship in Romney. The smuggling of brandy, silk and lace developed into a local industry on Romney Marsh.

Romney's decline as a port and the end of its prosperity came with the change in the course of the Rother. With no tidal flow, the course of the River Rother was changed towards Rye, which virtually made New Romney an isolated enclave. The great storm swept away three churches, and ships which had tied up to the walls of the Norman church of St Nicholas could no longer sail up the sluggish creek. The great Cinque Port of New Romney now became a small inland town.

Even so, the town continued to be a meeting place for the Cinque Port courts. New Romney is still considered to be the 'capital' of the Marsh, and today it has the feel of a quiet picturesque inland village. The Marshes around Romney measure some 17 miles long by 12 miles wide, some 46,000 acres, and the rich pastures give the name to the local breed of Romney Marsh sheep.

Dover

BY THE 21st century, Dover is the only one of the original Cinque Ports which has retained its importance as a port. This is obviously due to its position nearest to the French coast; this is why Dover was the first place that Julius Caesar made for when he crossed the Channel in 55 BC.

A thousand years later, the Lord Warden of the Cinque Ports had his residence in Dover Castle before relocating to Walmer Castle. Today, its improved road and rail links to London, its large artificial harbour and its modern roll-on roll-off Cross Channel ferries have strengthened Dover's strategic position. Today it is regarded as the 'Gateway to Britain', the world's busiest international passenger port.

By the time of the Confederation of the Cinque Ports, Dover had become a fairly large and prosperous town, with many ships and mariners enjoying considerable trade with the continent. When William the Conqueror invaded near Hastings in 1066, he needed Dover more than Dover needed him. He needed the Castle and the town, for they controlled his lifeline to France.

Dover, The Promenade 1924 76042

In 1217, one hundred French invading ships were seen off Dover; they were chased and defeated off North Foreland. After King John lost Normandy, the Dover Straits were no longer a bridge between two friendly countries, but instead became a battleground between two hostile nations.

Dover Castle withstood several sieges and raids, causing the outer walls to be strengthened and stronger entrance gates to be built. Amongst these were the Constable's Tower and Gate.

▶ **Dover, The White Cliffs 1897** 40714

▼ **Dover, General View c1955** D50011
Dover has always been dominated by its great castle on the eastern heights. For nearly two thousand years it has been a military stronghold, from when it was first built with earthen defences to its later imposing keep, towers and wide stone walls. It looks magnificently dramatic from any direction, whether from shipping in the Channel, from the town in its steep-sided valley below, or from the modern motorway to the east.

◀ **Dover
The Car Ferry
Terminal
c1965** D50069

Dover, The Castle, the Pharos c1965 D50103

Dover, The Church and the Pharos c1874 7081

Dover, The Castle Church and the Pharos 1892 31425

The Pharos, or Roman lighthouse, is a weatherworn shell whose top storey was rebuilt in the 15th century. The Romans erected it as a beacon for their galleys coming over from Gaul. Adjoining it is St Martins in the Castle, one of the most important pre-Conquest buildings surviving in this country, although much restored in 1862 and 1888. It became the Garrison church in 1267, a position it still retains today.

Dover, The Castle, the Constable's Tower and Gate 1890 25707
These defences were built in 1216 after the French siege of the castle had destroyed the old north gate. It was first known as Newgate; the tower was later enlarged in 1881. The outer perimeter walls were built during the 12th and 13th centuries, with towers at intervals in the walls. It is now the residence of the Deputy Governor, an Army appointment, and is the main entrance to the castle.

Dover, The Castle 1892 31419

The great castle keep, one of the most massive, complicated and impregnable in Europe, was built around 1190. The keep was divided horizontally into three floors, with two great halls, and was defended by walls varying from 16 to 25 feet in thickness. The whole of the castle was drastically remodelled during the Napoleonic Wars, when great barracks were erected. The castle remained an important base for the military authorities throughout both the World Wars.

In the heyday of the Cinque Ports, Dover featured prominently in ship service for the King. Time and again, Dover seamen were an important part of the Confederation in sea battles, starting with the complete defeat of a Danish raiding fleet off Dover and Sandwich in 1069.

Dover men also played a major role in the crusading fleet which captured Lisbon in 1147; they were also involved in the great victory of 1213, when hundreds of small French ships were sunk and over 200 were captured. Dover shipping also served in the great Battle of Sluys in 1340, and helped transport the King's armies across the Channel to the Battle of Crecy in 1346 and Agincourt in 1415. During these centuries, Dover had far-reaching powers of self-government and self-defence, and was responsible for its own taxation and the operation of law enforcement in its area.

Dover, The Harbour c1960 D50029
Dover had no natural harbour, and in early times ships would anchor offshore and load and unload through small boats. In Queen Elizabeth I's reign it was decided to build an enclosed harbour, and the Great Pent was constructed in 1583. The Wellington Dock was the larger successor to this first artificial harbour. During the 19th century, many enlargements and great constructional works were undertaken, including the Prince of Wales Pier, named in honour of the later Edward VII in 1902.

Dover, Admiralty Pier 1901 48058
Dover harbour had always suffered from the eastwards drift of shingle, and in Cinque Ports days it had been given Royal aid in preference to other ports to fight 'the eastern drift of shingle'. The building of the Admiralty Pier in 1871 helped to free the harbour from its blocking by shingle. This pier, part of a grand scheme to enclose the bay as a harbour of refuge, was 2100 feet long; it terminated in a revolving defence gun turret of two 81-ton guns. This vast area of enclosed water, the Great Admiralty Harbour of 1909, was designed for both naval and commercial roles. It provided an anchorage, should it be required, for 13 battleships, 14 cruisers and dozens of smaller naval craft. These waters are now given over to more commercial uses, including the accommodation of cruise liners.

◄ **Dover
From the
Castle 1906**
56936

◀ Dover, The Promenade Pier 1901 48060
(The Promenade Pier was opened in 1893, but over 100 feet of it was washed away the following year. In 1901 a pavilion was added at the end, but this failed dismally. In 1913 the pier was leased to the Admiralty as a landing stage. After the Great War it became a popular promenade with a concert hall at the seaward end; here, local steamers would unload tourists from Hastings, Deal and Thanet. Dover Pier fell into decay in the 1920s and was finally demolished in 1927.

**▼ Dover
The Promenade 1924**
76039

◀ Dover, Marine Parade 1892 31418
In 1816 the Harbour Commissioners decided to build houses on the shingle bank near the sea. The new fashion for seaside holidays and sea bathing in the 1830s provided an added impetus to many projects for seaside residences; the building of the Marine Parade in 1834 separated the houses from the beach. The long years of military threats from the Continent ended with England's victory at sea in the Battle of Trafalgar and on land from the victory at Waterloo in 1815. The Victorian spirit of optimism is shown by the construction work on the new Dover Promenade Pier (right).

Dover

**Dover, The Beach
1890** 25699
In Victorian and
Edwardian times, Dover
became fairly popular
as a minor seaside
resort. Holidaymakers
were always advised of
the ease of ferry trips to
France, at a time when
few people ventured
abroad. During the
Second World War this
whole area was affected
by the long-range
shelling of Dover by the
Germans, which began
in August 1940. The
last enemy shell fell in
September 1944, by
which time 10,056
premises in the town
had suffered damage.

▼ **Dover, The Beach 1908** 60396

▼ **Dover, The Gateway c1965** D50120

▲ **Dover, The Gateway c1965** D50086
Apart from the castle, an impressive area of Dover is the waterfront, where post-war reconstruction after the war damage resulted in the Gateway on a beautiful seafront site overlooking the harbour. A six-storey block containing 221 flats of varying sizes, it provides a striking introduction to the Gateway of Britain, for it is one of the first things that overseas visitors see on leaving the ferry port.

◀ **Dover, The Dover Stage
c1965** D50032
This hotel opened in 1957
to cater for modern
travellers in the same way
as the old inn here looked
after stage coach
passengers at a time when
the turnpike roads linked
London with the cross-
Channel shipping. The six-
storey building is supported
on concrete pillars in the
soft shingle subsoil.

▲ **Dover, Shakespeare Cliff 1908** 60413

◀ **Dover, Shakespeare Cliff 1887** 19984
This great white precipitous cliff, 350 feet high, takes its name from a passage in Shakespeare's 'King Lear'. This is said to be the site where Edgar brings the blinded Gloucester in the fourth act of 'King Lear', making him believe he has fallen over the edge and survived. The railway tunnel was cut in 1843; it leads through to Folkestone then on to London.

The loss of independent status for Dover as a Cinque Port, together with Deal and Sandwich, ended with local government re organisation in April 1974. They merged with local Rural and Urban District Councils to form the single unit of local government, the Dover District Council.

▲ **Dover, The Rolls Memorial c1965** D50088
The Hon Charles Rolls made the first two-way flight across the Channel without landing on 2 June 1910. Unfortunately, shortly afterwards he was killed in a flying accident, hence the memorial. On the cliff above this statue lies the landing field of Louis Bleriot, the Frenchman who made the first flight from France to England in July 1909.

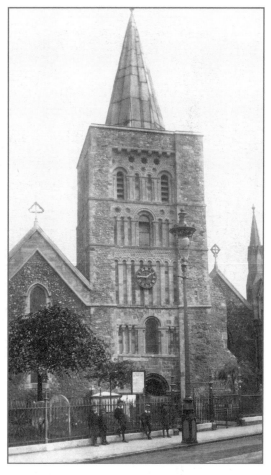

▲ **Dover, St Mary's Church 1899** 44803
St Mary's has been the parish church of Dover since 1585. The chapel of the Hospice of St Mary was probably the origin of the present church. St Mary's Hospice, built in 1203, was the leper hospital of the Maison Dieu. This was established in the late 11th century to provide food and shelter for travellers to and from the continent. The foundations and the lower walls of the church are early Norman, but St Mary's was completely rebuilt in 1843, with further restorations in 1897.

Sandwich

Sandwich, Old Houses 1924 76229

SANDWICH now lies several miles inland, but it was once a thriving port on the River Stour. As early as the 7th century, a trading centre had been established on a sandbank beside the harbour. This flourished throughout the next three centuries. In 1086, Sandwich had 383 houses and was the second largest town in Kent after Canterbury; it was a major port both for international trade and for entry and return to and from the Continent. By medieval times it had become one of the most important ports in the country. It was a key member of the Cinque Ports; it vied with Hastings as the most illustrious of the five coastal towns, its harbour busy with ships and merchants. It became England's chief naval and military port, and King Henry VII was once able to call on 95 ships with 1500 sailors for the King's service.

As Head Port of the Confederation, Sandwich played a leading part in the growth of England into a powerful nation from the time of the Norman invasion to its great explosion of power in Tudor times. Edward the Confessor established his residence in Sandwich in 1049, and made the harbour a base for his fleet. In 1052 he had 40 vessels fitted out while lying at Sandwich, and many raids were made on French ports. The Sandwich ships were smaller, crewed by just 21 men, and their main weapons were cross bows, arrows, grappling irons and swords, with quicklime to hurl into the enemy's faces. The French retaliated with a larger fleet, and in 1216 they pillaged Sandwich. The following year a sea battle took place in what became known as 'our first great British naval victory'.

In 1345 a fleet of 700 sail was raised by Edward III and sailed from Sandwich Haven for the Siege of Calais. Two years later, Sandwich provided the King with 22 ships manned by 504 men. The town continued to grow and prosper until the middle of the 15th century; by that time, England no longer had control of the narrow Straits of Dover, and the harbour was beginning to silt up. The decline came in 1457, when 4000 Frenchmen landed; they burnt and pillaged the buildings, and put most of the townsfolk to the sword. They killed the Mayor, whose successors ever since have worn a black robe on all ceremonial occasions. After that date, Sandwich never fully recovered its earlier prosperity, and the gradual silting-up of its channel at Pegwell Bay, coupled with the increasing size of commercial ships, eventually sounded the death knell to its seaborne trade.

Sandwich, An Old Cottage 1924 76231

Sandwich, The Weavers c1960 s60046
The name 'the Weavers' derives from Huguenot refugees, who fled from religious persecution in the Low Countries in the 1560s. They brought new prosperity through weaving cloth at a time when the harbour was silting up. A commercial enterprise opened in Strand Street in 1928, which has the finest of Sandwich's 17th century timber-framed houses; the panels within the timbering are filled with wattle and daub. Until recently the timber-framing had been plastered over, but it has now been revealed. The Dutch influence on the life of the town can still be seen in the number of Flemish gables and the well-preserved Dutch House in King Street. By 1600 the Dutch refugees and the weavers outnumbered the native-born inhabitants.

Sandwich, New Street c1955 S60001

Sandwich, The Admiral Owen c1955 S60014

Strand Street, which we see here, was originally the strand or foreshore when Sandwich was a port. The buildings stand entirely on reclaimed land, which was open water until the 14th century. Reclamation brought the shoreline forward, and a quay and warehouses were built. Even today, some vaulted store rooms of the medieval merchants still exist beneath some of the shops in this street. The Admiral Owen public house, with its 16th-century timbered overhanging storey, is named after a local admiral born in 1717, who captured large numbers of French gunboats in 1804, when Napoleon was planning to invade.

Sandwich, The Fishergate 1894 34209
The Fishergate is the only part of the fortifications still surviving. Built in 1384, it was one of the main entrances giving access to the town from the riverside wharves through the narrow and cobbled Quay Land, which led to the Custom House. Thomas Beckett would probably have walked along this lane when he landed at Sandwich a few days before his murder in Canterbury Cathedral.

Sandwich, The Fishergate 1914 67161

The Fishergate is built of flint; the upper storey was added in 1571. In Cinque Port days, this quay would often be crowded with the royal household and its horses and baggage waiting to embark for France. The Ship Inn, to the left of the gate, was renamed the Admiral Rodney in the 18th century; it is now a private house.

▼ Sandwich, The Barbican 1894 34210

This is one of a chain of blockhouses built in 1539 by Henry VIII when Deal, Walmer and Sandown Castles were constructed as part of our coastal defences. Fine flint and stone chequers decorate the base. Originally this was not a proper gateway to Sandwich, but part of the outer defensive works. Once known as Daveysgate, it later became the residence of the keepers of the toll bridge.

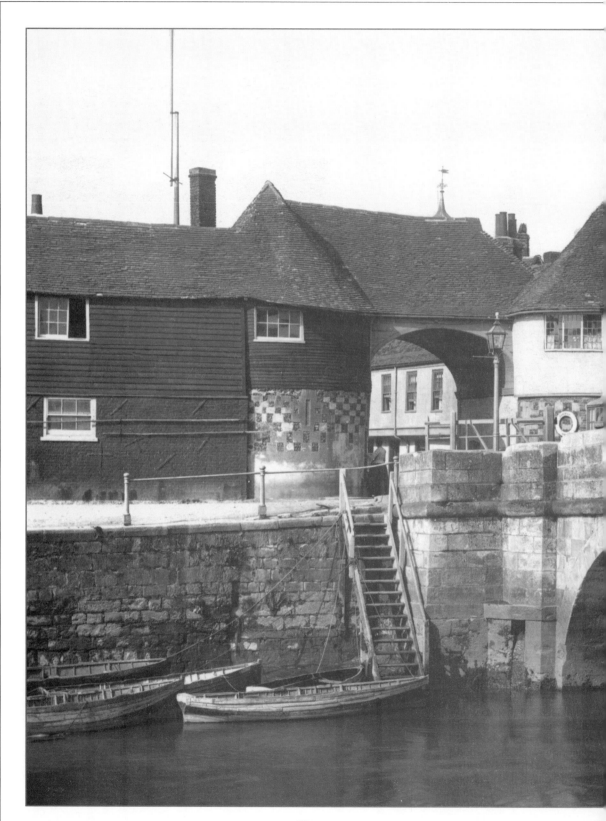

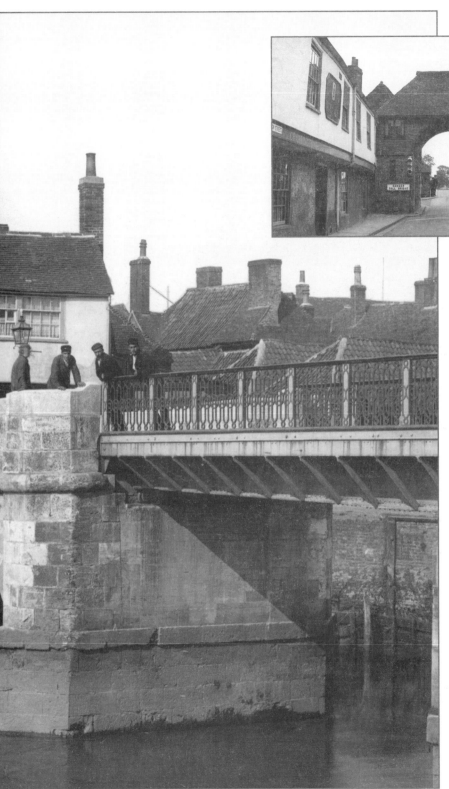

**▲ Sandwich
The Barbican c1955**
S60010

**◄ Sandwich
The Barbican
and the Bridge 1894**
34212

From 1290, this was the site of the inconvenient ferry across the Stour. In 1757 a wooden drawbridge was built; this became unsafe and was replaced in 1839 by a swing bridge to permit river-borne traffic to proceed up river. This in turn was replaced by the existing bridge in 1891. Complicated tolls were imposed for the upkeep of the bridge, but after 1786 the money received was devoted to expenditure on public works in Sandwich. With the building of the new bypass in 1977, the tolls were discontinued.

▼ **Sandwich, St Clement's Church 1894** 34207

St Clement's is the largest church in Sandwich, the oldest part being the massive central tower of Caen stone built around 1100. In 1634 this church was reserved for the use of some 500 Dutch residents who had fled from religious persecution abroad.

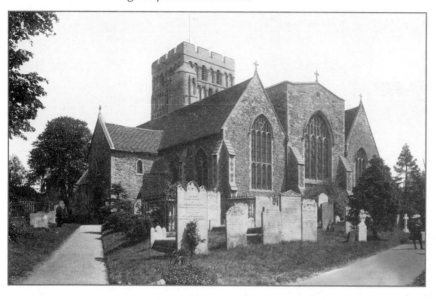

▼ **Sandwich, St Peter's Church 1894** 34208

This church stands in the centre of Sandwich; it was erected about 1200 by Norman monks, and was enlarged in the 13th century when the tower was added. In 1661 the tower and much of the church fell down. It was rebuilt in brick, and the tower was topped by a cupola, which gave it a Dutch appearance.

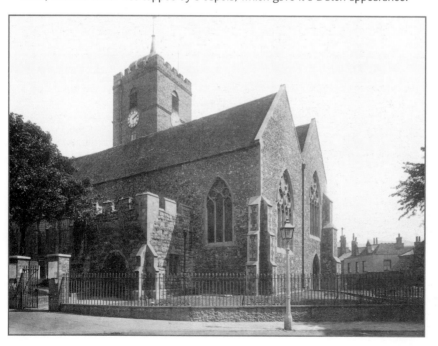

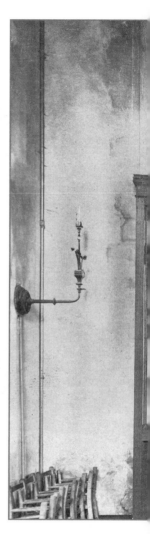

▲ **Sandwich, St Clement's Church 1924** 76240

As Sandwich grew, so St Clement's was enlarged, until it attained its present size after several restorations in the 19th century. The Mayor was elected here in the past, and a traditional Mayor's procession takes place on the first Sunday following his election. St Clement's was designated as the Parish Church in 1948, when the three Sandwich parishes were combined.

◀ **Sandwich, St Peter's Church 1924** 76237
From the 13th century until the Second World War a curfew used to be rung every night at 8pm. It was rung by a team of 31 volunteers from the town, each with his own day of the month. The old church clock was replaced in 1887 as part of the celebrations for Queen Victoria's Golden Jubilee. St Peter's is now empty, and is under the care of the Redundant Church Commission.

▶ **Sandwich, The Rope Walk c1955** S60005
This area of pleasant shady walks was recorded in 1431 as 'a sporting place for the archers'. From these butts, Henry V's archers who fought on the battlefields of Agincourt and Crecy are said to have practised with their longbows. In Cinque Port days, Gallows Field to the right was the area where according to Port law murderers were buried alive, and suspected witches were drowned in the Guestling Stream.

◀ **Sandwich, The Rope Walk c1955**
S60004
By the 14th century, most of the Cinque Ports were protected by walls or ramparts as a defence against the merciless enemy across the Channel. It is to this period that the high embankment and ditch called the Rope Walk belong. There were stone walls and gates on the harbour and river side, and earthen defences on the land side. The water to the right became the 'town ditch', while the Rope Walk was used for making ropes for the many sailing vessels which traded here before the haven silted up.

Sandwich, The Guildhall c1960 s60034

The Guildhall was built in 1579 in the north-east corner of the Cattle Market. Extensive renovations took place in 1912, and the original building was modernised with a half-timbered facade. In 1972 further extensions were added, which give the building a slightly bogus look. The Courtroom with its fine wooden panelling has been used continuously for the administration of justice from 1579 to 1987, when the Magistrates' Court moved to Dover.

Sandwich, The King's House 1924 76234

The King's House is a fine timber-framed Tudor building with later 18th-century additions. It gets its name because Henry VIII lodged here when he was concerned at the silting up of Sandwich Haven in 1532 and 1539. Fresh hopes were raised when Queen Elizabeth also stayed here when she visited Sandwich in 1573. Although the Queen ate some of the banquet of 160 dishes and was 'very merry', it is recorded that she did nothing at all about a petition to clear the harbour, now being progressively blocked by the sea sand. In the foreground is the river waterfront, which in the past was the landing area for goods unloaded from the timber wharves.

Sandwich, The Pilgrim's House 1924 76230
The Pilgrim's House, No 39 Strand Street, had its origins in Norman times when it stood on the quayside fronting the river. Over the years various additions were made, and even the present facade dates back well over 400 years. Records showing that this house was used for travelling pilgrims go well back into the Middle Ages. Before the Second World War it became Sir Oswald Mosley's headquarters in his attempt to establish a Fascist presence in East Kent, but he never achieved any success.

**Sandwich
The River 1924** 76227
A small coastal trade
still existed before the
advent of the railway.
Regular services to and
from London and other
ports carried coal, salt,
timber, cement and
other bulk
commodities.

Sandwich, The Guilford Hotel c1955 S60029

The flat land outside Sandwich left by the receding sea were admirably adapted to golf links, notably the Royal St Georges, founded in 1887, and later the Princes. The hotel named after the Earl of Guilford was built as a luxury hotel in 1912, and became a haven for many thousands of golfers enjoying the excellent facilities. A special railway was built across the marshes to carry the materials for its construction. The Guilford Hotel was finally demolished in the 1970s.

With the passing of the centuries, the port of Sandwich gradually silted up as the sea slowly receded. Sandwich is now two miles from the sea as the crow flies, yet the sluggish meanders of the Stour mean that any vessel passing up river to tie up at Sandwich Quay must make a trip of nearly eight miles.

Sandwich, The River and the Bridge c1960 S60048

The last twenty years have seen a large industrial estate develop outside the town, so that the old Cinque Port that once fed the monks of Canterbury with 40,000 herrings a year now produces drugs, pharmaceutical medicines, rubber appliances and machine parts for the nation.

Sandwich, The River and the Bridge c1960 S60047
Today, little has changed in Sandwich; its attractive tangle of medieval streets and buildings are jealously preserved and maintained. The population now stands at 4590, probably little more now than it was during its heyday as a Cinque Port. This tranquil river scene belies the importance of Sandwich as a port in the history of the English nation some six hundred years earlier.

THE TWO ANCIENT TOWNS

Rye & Winchelsea

BY THE 12th century, the increase in ship services demanded by the Crown was found to be too great for the original five Cinque Ports of Hastings, Romney, Hythe, Dover and Sandwich to carry out successfully, so it was necessary to add new members. Two ports, Rye and Winchelsea, at first attached to Hastings, had become so prosperous and important that they were given Head Port status, having complete equality in all respects with the original five. Rye was already a borough before the Domesday survey, and King Stephen had set up a mint here in 1141. With the addition of Rye and Winchelsea, the Confederation of the Cinque Ports took the new title of 'The Cinque Ports and the two Ancient Towns', the name by which it is still known today.

Rye, Lion Street 1903 51078
Today, Rye is a picturesque ensemble of Georgian houses, old inns, fortifications and hilly streets. Lion Street has a mixture of frontages, with some shops bow-windowed and some weatherboarded. St Mary's parish church on the crest of the hill dominates the street, and has a church clock which only strikes the quarters, not the hours.

The ancient settlement of Rye developed around the time of the Norman Conquest, when the Abbey of Fecamp in Normandy owned the site with its small harbour – at that time the sea flowed right up to the sandstone cliffs. Rye prospered later than the other Cinque Ports. It reached its greatest importance in the 13th and first half of the 14th centuries, when it was a thriving port with a fishing fleet, a market place, and a wharf where the King's galleys were docked and repaired.

The change in Rye's fortunes came mainly through the tremendous storm of 1287, which altered the coastline and changed the course of the Rother and the smaller rivers; at their confluence, these had once provided an excellent harbour south of the town. In 1289 Rye was raised to the status of a Borough and contributed 5 ships to the confederation, as many as Hythe, Sandwich and Romney.

The receding sea and the consequent silting affected Rye much later than some of the other ports, but it was the French, not the sea, that really finished Rye. The French had made Rye one of their chief targets, and havoc and death came one terrible night in 1377, when the town was completely burnt to the ground. After the French attack, some of the inhabitants were held responsible for their failure to protect the town and were executed as traitors. Richard I gave leave to the Barons of the Cinque Ports 'to enclose and strengthen the town with strong walls and gates'.

During the next two centuries, Rye managed a slight recovery, but the constant problems of the relentless silting of the former wide harbour and estuary prevented the town from ever again approaching its former status. Surrounding marshland was reclaimed to the east and north-east, and the volume of tidal waters in and out of Rye Bay was enormously reduced.

Rye, From the North 1890 25401

Rye, West Cliff 1888 21145

Rye, The Church 1890 25406

▼ **Rye, Battery Garden, Ypres Castle 1901** 47450

Ypres Tower was built in 1135; originally called Buddings Tower, it was once part of Rye's defences. When Rye became impoverished in 1430, it was sold to a Norman family, John de Ypres, thus acquiring its present name. After Dover Castle, Ypres Tower is the oldest fortification remaining in any of the Cinque Ports. Since Tudor times, the Tower has belonged to the Corporation, which held its meetings here until the Commonwealth. It is now the Town Museum.

The Battery Garden, or Gun Garden, adjoining the Ypres Tower on the hill offers wide prospects seawards over the drained marshlands. In Elizabethan times it was recorded that 'Her Majesty's ordnance threatened the sheep and seagulls on the flats below'.

▲ **Rye, Ypres Tower 1901** 47451

◄ **Rye, From the South-West 1890** 25403

Rye, Mermaid Street 1901 47454
This is a narrow, steep cobbled street faced with a pleasant variety of old buildings. The half-timbered Hartshorn House to the right has a restored facade with overhanging gables dating from 1576 and leaded windows typical of this period. It was once a hospital, and housed sick soldiers in the Napoleonic Wars.

Rye, The Oldest Houses 1901 47457

Rye, The Mermaid Hotel c1955 R77030

Rye, The Mermaid Hotel 1901 47456
This inn, one of the 17 public houses in Rye, dates back to Tudor times; it is a haven for travellers across country. The archway in the centre leads into the courtyard and stabling for the stage-coach horses. The hotel has a vaulted undercroft, which was used as a storehouse by the smuggling gangs of the marshes. The Mermaid has welcomed the sundry anniversaries of royal birthdays, national victories and civic functions over the centuries.

▼ **Rye, Lamb House and Henry James' Study 1925** 77238
Henry James, the expatriate American novelist, fell in love with Rye, and lived
and wrote in the Georgian red-brick Lamb House from 1897 until his death in
1916. James Lamb, a former Mayor, founded a family which ran Rye for over a
century. The building is now owned by the National Trust.

▲ **Rye, The Landgate
1925** 77240
This is one of the few
surviving town gateways
in Sussex. It is the only
one remaining of the four
gates to Rye, and
provided defence on the
landward side. Built
between 1340 and 1385,
it was originally provided
with a drawbridge and a
portcullis; it had gates
which would be closed at
dusk each day.

▶ **Rye, East Cliff 1906**
53475

◀ **Rye, Romney Marshes c1955** R77102
Today, the River Rother takes a long curving course to the south-east of the town and joins the open sea nearly three miles away. Despite all the reclamation of the marshland, Rye was fortunate that the Rother did not entirely desert her; a fragmented community taking the name Rye Harbour has grown up two miles nearer the sea.

▶ **Rye, The Hill and the River Rother 1901** 47447

▼ **Rye, The Hill 1901** 47448

▲ **Rye, The River Rother 1901** 47445

◀ **Rye, The Harbour c1955** R77005

The quay is the historic seafaring mercantile area of the town. In the past, barges would sail up to Rye with cargoes of timber from the Baltic and coal from the Tyne. With the volume of tidal waters ever decreasing, nowadays a cargo of any type rarely comes up the River Rother, other than small individual fishing craft.

Rye, The Harbour c1955 R77006

Rye, The Harbour c1955 R77059
Reports from the late 19th century show that at least 50 fishing vessels were registered as using Rye harbour, situated some two miles south of Rye at the narrow and awkward mouth of the Rother. Today it retains limited popularity as the unsophisticated haunt of small boat owners.

Rye, Camber Castle Keep 1894 34447
To the south of Rye Harbour stand the low rounded walls of Camber Castle, now stranded helplessly inland from the sea. Like other castles round the south-east coast, Camber was one of a chain of castles built as a national defence against the invasion threat of the 1530s.

VISITING the attractive and well-cared-for small town of Winchelsea, it is difficult to imagine that once it was a leading town of England and the major port of Sussex. Its history is closely bound with the history of the Cinque Ports. From its sandstone outcrop it controlled the western entrance to the wide bay. It was always affected by the local wave and wind currents which tended to drive shingle and sand eastwards, hence the year-by-year growth of Dungeness.

Winchelsea was not originally sited on the rising ground where it now stands, but on a shingle spit running north-east from the Fairlight Cliffs, where an important wine trade with France grew up in 1130. This original site has now been engulfed by the sea, and historians still disagree as to its exact position.

This old town site was prone to disaster over the years. Exposed to fires and damage from French raids, it was also often inundated by the sea storms on a number of occasions between 1236 and 1252. With each flooding, more and more of the shingle spit on which the town was built was washed away. Old Winchelsea steadily became less and less habitable. Eventually a catastrophic storm in 1287 resulted in so much damage that the town became unfit for habitation. All the townspeople could do was to abandon the site completely and move to higher ground.

Winchelsea, The Town 1906 53490
Winchelsea was one of England's first examples of town planning. After Old Winchelsea was flooded out in 1250 and again in 1287, it was re-sited on the higher outcrop of sandstone. Edward I instigated the plan for the town's rebuilding. A rigid grid of streets was laid out: four streets by four streets at right angles. The rectangular house plots were offered rent free for seven years to migrants from the flooded Old Town.

A few years later saw the rise in importance of Winchelsea when the new town became an important addition to the Confederation of the Cinque Ports and the Two Ancient Towns. During this period, Winchelsea was sending 21 ships manned by 596 seamen, even eclipsing Dover's quota of 16 ships and 336 men.

King Edward I personally provided the land for its present site on the sandstone hill. He divided the new town into rigid blocks of streets at right angles to each other, a medieval example of some of our earliest town planning. By 1292, New Winchelsea was finally occupied by the resettled migrants.

For the next two centuries, Winchelsea on its hill prospered greatly; but there was always an uneven struggle between land and sea influences. Besides the fishing, local seamen were often engaged in piracy, and in the early 14th century the town was charged with six cases of piracy in the Straits of Dover, despite supplying two ships to the Crown to suppress all piracy.

For the Siege of Calais in 1347, Winchelsea sent 21 ships to the Cinque Ports fleet of 105 vessels with 2140 men. Although Winchelsea was now safe from flooding from the sea, it was still vulnerable to enemy raids by the French. In retaliation, the French attacked the town in 1359 and left the parish church of St Thomas in ruins.

Gradually Winchelsea declined in prestige, though it always remained a hot bed of the smuggling gangs on Romney Marsh. The town still has numerous stone-vaulted cellars, or undercrofts, as storehouses for smuggled goods under much later buildings.

The receding sea, the silting up of the harbour through the eastward drift of shingle, the Black Death, and intermittent French raids, all hastened Winchelsea's decline. By the 16th century there was no access by ship to Winchelsea, and the town ceased to be a port.

The town has now developed its own particular charm, with an intriguing mix of medieval, Georgian, Victorian and modern buildings, but still little visited by tourists. Whereas the other ancient Cinque Port town of Rye seethes with tourist bustle, in Winchelsea all is quiet, with hardly a shop to be seen among the few tranquil streets of red brick and weatherboarding.

Winchelsea, From Rye Road 1906 53482

Winchelsea, High Street from Strand Gate c1960 W106006

Winchelsea, Queen Elizabeth's Well 1906 53486

▲ **Winchelsea, Strand Gate 1894** 34448

◀ **Winchelsea, Strand Gate c1955** W106005

Here we see the impressive rounded corner gates of the Strand Gate. This was one of the original gates surviving from this now shrunken medieval town.

◄ **Winchelsea
Castle Street
c1960** W10601

◄ Winchelsea, St Thomas's Church 1894
34449

The impressive church of St Thomas was partly destroyed in a French raid of 1359. All that now remains of this once cathedral-like building are the ruined walls of the choir and side chapel. The tall west tower and nave were destroyed in a later French attack in 1459.

▼ Winchelsea St Thomas's Church 1888 21178

◄ Winchelsea, The New Gate 1906 53484

This is possibly Winchelsea's loneliest and most evocative ruin, the New Gate. It was through this gate that the French were treacherously admitted in 1380. One may imagine them pillaging and burning their way through the town, leaving devastated areas now covered by open grass spaces. Adjoining the gate is the deep defensive town ditch.

Winchelsea, The Friars 1888 21182
These are the ivy-covered remains of the ruined chancel arch and choir of the Grey Friars religious community; they stand opposite the fields that were once the town's market place in more prosperous times.

Winchelsea, The Friars 1906 53487

Winchelsea, The Court Hall 1894 34452
The lower floor was once the town gaol, while the Town Museum now occupies the upper floor. Here are boards painted with the names of Mayors of Winchelsea since 1295. Winchelsea is said to be the smallest town in the country to have its own Mayor and Corporation.

Winchelsea, The Armoury c1960 W106009

The Seven Corporate Members or 'Limbs'

The loss of Normandy in 1204 imposed a severe strain on the resources of the original Cinque Ports Confederation, so they enlisted the help of nearby towns and villages. These additional settlements helped to relieve the pressure on the Head Ports for supplying ships, manpower and money to the King. Consequently the Head Ports enlisted 7 corporate members known as 'limbs', and thus became the centre of a group of associated towns, making 14 in all.

These alliances were obviously beneficial to both parties. The 7 Head Ports enlarged their influence within the Confederation, while the 7 'limbs' obtained considerable benefit through the extension of many liberties and privileges, giving them complete equality with the Head Port to which they were attached. The only ports without a

Folkestone, The Leas 1940 F35001
Folkestone was a fashionable resort from Victorian times. A stroll along the Leas on the cliff top was an attraction to visitors happy to enjoy a quiet holiday.

corporate member were Hythe and Winchelsea, while Romney just had an association with Lydd. The other four Head Ports were supported by other nearby communities, as we shall see below.

Dover enlisted Folkestone in the first half of the 13th century. Its other 'limb' was Faversham, which joined in 1252. For centuries Faversham was a prosperous coastal port, important for its building of small sailing vessels. A fleet was sent to support Dover through the 13th and 14th centuries, while Dover often supported Faversham in its continual state of warfare with successive Abbots of Faversham.

Sandwich enlisted Fordwich, Deal and Walmer as its 'limbs'.

Some of the 'limbs' previously described became larger and more important then the particular Head Port to which they were attached, but none were ever permitted to become Head Ports in the Confederation. Towards the end of the 14th century, each of the

Corporate 'limbs' annexed neighbouring communities in the same way as they were acquired to help them fulfil their quota of ships, men and victuals. These extra settlements were added to the Cinque Ports as 'Non-Corporate Members'. Ultimately there were some 30 towns and villages which gave help to the Cinque Port Confederation. Included in this group were Ramsgate, Sarre and Brightlingsea (for Sandwich), Margate, Birchington, St Peters and Kingsdown (for Dover), Hidney, Beckesbourne and Grange (for Hastings), and Old Romney, Dungemarsh and Oswaldstone (for Romney).

Unfortunately, due to the vague and controversial recording of the times, some authorities dispute the number of settlements involved in aiding the country against seaborne invasion. The documents definitely record some 30 towns actively involved in the Cinque Ports Confederation, although some historic lists mention at least 42 settlements.

Folkestone, General View 1901 48048
Until the growth of the seaside resort on the cliff top, Folkestone was merely a huddle of fishermen's cottages around the harbour.

Folkestone, The Town Hall 1965 F35172
This solid-looking Town Hall, built towards the turn of the century, is indicative of the increasing prosperity brought by the important ferry link with Boulogne in France.

Faversham, The Town Hall 1960 F13046
Faversham has a wealth of historical buildings, including the wooden-arched Guildhall of 1574, which now supports the Town Hall of 1814 on the upper floor.

▼ Fordwich, The Village c1955 F38016

For over a millennium, Fordwich was the port for Canterbury at a time when the Stour was wider and deeper than it is today. French stone from Caen for the construction of the cathedral was landed here.

▼ Fordwich, The Maltings c1955 F38005

Fordwich was the only Merchant Guild in the Cinque Port Confederation, and Sandwich allowed the port to drown criminals in the Stour, with a ducking stool for minor offences. Fordwich declined in importance during the Middle Ages through the increasing silting, decreasing width and absence of tidal flow in the river.

▲ Walmer, St Mary's Church 1924 76077

Walmer joined the Confederation in 1353, when it had a fishing fleet of small vessels manned by skilful seamen.

◄ **Walmer, The Castle Grounds 1906** 56932 Walmer Castle was built as a defence against invasion by Henry VIII in 1539/40, and since then it has been the residence of the Lord Warden of the Cinque Ports, a post occupied for many years by our Queen Mother.

◄ **Walmer, The Strand c1955** W12003
The town is now a popular residential and holiday area, with its long strand facing the treacherous Goodwin Sands. Records show that often as many as 400 sailing vessels would shelter offshore.

◄ Deal, Pier Parade 1906 56913

As a corporate 'limb' of Sandwich, Deal grew in importance as Sandwich fell into decline through increasing silting of the Stour. By the 19th century, Deal had developed into a minor seaside resort with a newly-constructed pier, and was well-known for its national fishing competitions.

▼ Deal, The View Looking South 1924 76046

Deal became a Cinque Port 'limb' in 1229; it was unique in that it was an important port without any harbour or berthing facilities. In the late 13th century, the local Deal fleet defeated superior French forces partly by throwing lime into the faces of boarding parties.

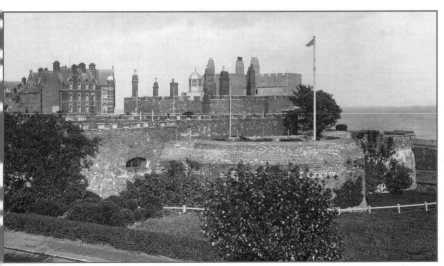

◄ Deal, The Castle 1924 76074

In 1539/40, Henry VIII feared invasion by the French or Spanish, so he built the three defensive castles of Deal, Walmer and Sandown along this area of coast.

Ramsgate, The Quay and the Harbour 1918 68462
Now a developing freight ferry cross-Channel port, Ramsgate assisted Sandwich when the original Head Cinque Port fell into decline through receding sea and increasing silting.

Ramsgate, The Pavilion from the Pier 1906 53467
With the arrival of the railway from London in 1846, Ramsgate developed its fishing industry, and later expanded into a popular seaside resort with a marina and cross-Channel ferry facilities.

Index

Frith Book Co Titles

www.francisfrith.co.uk

The Frith Book Company publishes over 100 new titles each year. A selection of those currently available are listed below. For latest catalogue please contact Frith Book Co.

Town Books 96 pages, approx 100 photos. County and Themed Books 128 pages, approx 150 photos (unless specified). All titles hardback laminated case and jacket except those indicated pb (paperback)

Amersham, Chesham & Rickmansworth (pb)	1-85937-340-2	£9.99
Ancient Monuments & Stone Circles	1-85937-143-4	£17.99
Aylesbury (pb)	1-85937-227-9	£9.99
Bakewell	1-85937-113-2	£12.99
Barnstaple (pb)	1-85937-300-3	£9.99
Bath (pb)	1-85937419-0	£9.99
Bedford (pb)	1-85937-205-8	£9.99
Berkshire (pb)	1-85937-191-4	£9.99
Berkshire Churches	1-85937-170-1	£17.99
Blackpool (pb)	1-85937-382-8	£9.99
Bognor Regis (pb)	1-85937-431-x	£9.99
Bournemouth	1-85937-067-5	£12.99
Bradford (pb)	1-85937-204-x	£9.99
Brighton & Hove(pb)	1-85937-192-2	£8.99
Bristol (pb)	1-85937-264-3	£9.99
British Life A Century Ago (pb)	1-85937-213-9	£9.99
Buckinghamshire (pb)	1-85937-200-7	£9.99
Camberley (pb)	1-85937-222-8	£9.99
Cambridge (pb)	1-85937-422-0	£9.99
Cambridgeshire (pb)	1-85937-420-4	£9.99
Canals & Waterways (pb)	1-85937-291-0	£9.99
Canterbury Cathedral (pb)	1-85937-179-5	£9.99
Cardiff (pb)	1-85937-093-4	£9.99
Carmarthenshire	1-85937-216-3	£14.99
Chelmsford (pb)	1-85937-310-0	£9.99
Cheltenham (pb)	1-85937-095-0	£9.99
Cheshire (pb)	1-85937-271-6	£9.99
Chester	1-85937-090-x	£12.99
Chesterfield	1-85937-378-x	£9.99
Chichester (pb)	1-85937-228-7	£9.99
Colchester (pb)	1-85937-188-4	£8.99
Cornish Coast	1-85937-163-9	£14.99
Cornwall (pb)	1-85937-229-5	£9.99
Cornwall Living Memories	1-85937-248-1	£14.99
Cotswolds (pb)	1-85937-230-9	£9.99
Cotswolds Living Memories	1-85937-255-4	£14.99
County Durham	1-85937-123-x	£14.99
Croydon Living Memories	1-85937-162-0	£9.99
Cumbria	1-85937-101-9	£14.99
Dartmoor	1-85937-145-0	£14.99
Derby (pb)	1-85937-367-4	£9.99
Derbyshire (pb)	1-85937-196-5	£9.99
Devon (pb)	1-85937-297-x	£9.99
Dorset (pb)	1-85937-269-4	£9.99
Dorset Churches	1-85937-172-8	£17.99
Dorset Coast (pb)	1-85937-299-6	£9.99
Dorset Living Memories	1-85937-210-4	£14.99
Down the Severn	1-85937-118-3	£14.99
Down the Thames (pb)	1-85937-278-3	£9.99
Down the Trent	1-85937-311-9	£14.99
Dublin (pb)	1-85937-231-7	£9.99
East Anglia (pb)	1-85937-265-1	£9.99
East London	1-85937-080-2	£14.99
East Sussex	1-85937-130-2	£14.99
Eastbourne	1-85937-061-6	£12.99
Edinburgh (pb)	1-85937-193-0	£8.99
England in the 1880s	1-85937-331-3	£17.99
English Castles (pb)	1-85937-434-4	£9.99
English Country Houses	1-85937-161-2	£17.99
Essex (pb)	1-85937-270-8	£9.99
Exeter	1-85937-126-4	£12.99
Exmoor	1-85937-132-9	£14.99
Falmouth	1-85937-066-7	£12.99
Folkestone (pb)	1-85937-124-8	£9.99
Glasgow (pb)	1-85937-190-6	£9.99
Gloucestershire	1-85937-102-7	£14.99
Great Yarmouth (pb)	1-85937-426-3	£9.99
Greater Manchester (pb)	1-85937-266-x	£9.99
Guildford (pb)	1-85937-410-7	£9.99
Hampshire (pb)	1-85937-279-1	£9.99
Hampshire Churches (pb)	1-85937-207-4	£9.99
Harrogate	1-85937-423-9	£9.99
Hastings & Bexhill (pb)	1-85937-131-0	£9.99
Heart of Lancashire (pb)	1-85937-197-3	£9.99
Helston (pb)	1-85937-214-7	£9.99
Hereford (pb)	1-85937-175-2	£9.99
Herefordshire	1-85937-174-4	£14.99
Hertfordshire (pb)	1-85937-247-3	£9.99
Horsham (pb)	1-85937-432-8	£9.99
Humberside	1-85937-215-5	£14.99
Hythe, Romney Marsh & Ashford	1-85937-256-2	£9.99

Available from your local bookshop or from the publisher

Frith Book Co Titles (continued)

Title	ISBN	Price	Title	ISBN	Price
Ipswich (pb)	1-85937-424-7	£9.99	St Ives (pb)	1-85937415-8	£9.99
Ireland (pb)	1-85937-181-7	£9.99	Scotland (pb)	1-85937-182-5	£9.99
Isle of Man (pb)	1-85937-268-6	£9.99	Scottish Castles (pb)	1-85937-323-2	£9.99
Isles of Scilly	1-85937-136-1	£14.99	Sevenoaks & Tunbridge	1-85937-057-8	£12.99
Isle of Wight (pb)	1-85937-429-8	£9.99	Sheffield, South Yorks (pb)	1-85937-267-8	£9.99
Isle of Wight Living Memories	1-85937-304-6	£14.99	Shrewsbury (pb)	1-85937-325-9	£9.99
Kent (pb)	1-85937-189-2	£9.99	Shropshire (pb)	1-85937-326-7	£9.99
Kent Living Memories	1-85937-125-6	£14.99	Somerset	1-85937-153-1	£14.99
Lake District (pb)	1-85937-275-9	£9.99	South Devon Coast	1-85937-107-8	£14.99
Lancaster, Morecambe & Heysham (pb)	1-85937-233-3	£9.99	South Devon Living Memories	1-85937-168-x	£14.99
Leeds (pb)	1-85937-202-3	£9.99	South Hams	1-85937-220-1	£14.99
Leicester	1-85937-073-x	£12.99	Southampton (pb)	1-85937-427-1	£9.99
Leicestershire (pb)	1-85937-185-x	£9.99	Southport (pb)	1-85937-425-5	£9.99
Lincolnshire (pb)	1-85937-433-6	£9.99	Staffordshire	1-85937-047-0	£12.99
Liverpool & Merseyside (pb)	1-85937-234-1	£9.99	Stratford upon Avon	1-85937-098-5	£12.99
London (pb)	1-85937-183-3	£9.99	Suffolk (pb)	1-85937-221-x	£9.99
Ludlow (pb)	1-85937-176-0	£9.99	Suffolk Coast	1-85937-259-7	£14.99
Luton (pb)	1-85937-235-x	£9.99	Surrey (pb)	1-85937-240-6	£9.99
Maidstone	1-85937-056-x	£14.99	Sussex (pb)	1-85937-184-1	£9.99
Manchester (pb)	1-85937-198-1	£9.99	Swansea (pb)	1-85937-167-1	£9.99
Middlesex	1-85937-158-2	£14.99	Tees Valley & Cleveland	1-85937-211-2	£14.99
New Forest	1-85937-128-0	£14.99	Thanet (pb)	1-85937-116-7	£9.99
Newark (pb)	1-85937-366-6	£9.99	Tiverton (pb)	1-85937-178-7	£9.99
Newport, Wales (pb)	1-85937-258-9	£9.99	Torbay	1-85937-063-2	£12.99
Newquay (pb)	1-85937-421-2	£9.99	Truro	1-85937-147-7	£12.99
Norfolk (pb)	1-85937-195-7	£9.99	Victorian and Edwardian Cornwall	1-85937-252-x	£14.99
Norfolk Living Memories	1-85937-217-1	£14.99	Victorian & Edwardian Devon	1-85937-253-8	£14.99
Northamptonshire	1-85937-150-7	£14.99	Victorian & Edwardian Kent	1-85937-149-3	£14.99
Northumberland Tyne & Wear (pb)	1-85937-281-3	£9.99	Vic & Ed Maritime Album	1-85937-144-2	£17.99
North Devon Coast	1-85937-146-9	£14.99	Victorian and Edwardian Sussex	1-85937-157-4	£14.99
North Devon Living Memories	1-85937-261-9	£14.99	Victorian & Edwardian Yorkshire	1-85937-154-x	£14.99
North London	1-85937-206-6	£14.99	Victorian Seaside	1-85937-159-0	£17.99
North Wales (pb)	1-85937-298-8	£9.99	Villages of Devon (pb)	1-85937-293-7	£9.99
North Yorkshire (pb)	1-85937-236-8	£9.99	Villages of Kent (pb)	1-85937-294-5	£9.99
Norwich (pb)	1-85937-194-9	£8.99	Villages of Sussex (pb)	1-85937-295-3	£9.99
Nottingham (pb)	1-85937-324-0	£9.99	Warwickshire (pb)	1-85937-203-1	£9.99
Nottinghamshire (pb)	1-85937-187-6	£9.99	Welsh Castles (pb)	1-85937-322-4	£9.99
Oxford (pb)	1-85937-411-5	£9.99	West Midlands (pb)	1-85937-289-9	£9.99
Oxfordshire (pb)	1-85937-430-1	£9.99	West Sussex	1-85937-148-5	£14.99
Peak District (pb)	1-85937-280-5	£9.99	West Yorkshire (pb)	1-85937-201-5	£9.99
Penzance	1-85937-069-1	£12.99	Weymouth (pb)	1-85937-209-0	£9.99
Peterborough (pb)	1-85937-219-8	£9.99	Wiltshire (pb)	1-85937-277-5	£9.99
Piers	1-85937-237-6	£17.99	Wiltshire Churches (pb)	1-85937-171-x	£9.99
Plymouth	1-85937-119-1	£12.99	Wiltshire Living Memories	1-85937-245-7	£14.99
Poole & Sandbanks (pb)	1-85937-251-1	£9.99	Winchester (pb)	1-85937-428-x	£9.99
Preston (pb)	1-85937-212-0	£9.99	Windmills & Watermills	1-85937-242-2	£17.99
Reading (pb)	1-85937-238-4	£9.99	Worcester (pb)	1-85937-165-5	£9.99
Romford (pb)	1-85937-319-4	£9.99	Worcestershire	1-85937-152-3	£14.99
Salisbury (pb)	1-85937-239-2	£9.99	York (pb)	1-85937-199-x	£9.99
Scarborough (pb)	1-85937-379-8	£9.99	Yorkshire (pb)	1-85937-186-8	£9.99
St Albans (pb)	1-85937-341-0	£9.99	Yorkshire Living Memories	1-85937-166-3	£14.99

See Frith books on the internet www.francisfrith.co.uk

FRITH PRODUCTS & SERVICES

Francis Frith would doubtless be pleased to know that the pioneering publishing venture he started in 1860 still continues today. A hundred and forty years later, The Francis Frith Collection continues in the same innovative tradition and is now one of the foremost publishers of vintage photographs in the world. Some of the current activities include:

Interior Decoration

Today Frith's photographs can be seen framed and as giant wall murals in thousands of pubs, restaurants, hotels, banks, retail stores and other public buildings throughout the country. In every case they enhance the unique local atmosphere of the places they depict and provide reminders of gentler days in an increasingly busy and frenetic world.

Product Promotions

Frith products are used by many major companies to promote the sales of their own products or to reinforce their own history and heritage. Frith promotions have been used by Hovis bread, Courage beers, Scots Porage Oats, Colman's mustard, Cadbury's foods, Mellow Birds coffee, Dunhill pipe tobacco, Guinness, and Bulmer's Cider.

Genealogy and Family History

As the interest in family history and roots grows world-wide, more and more people are turning to Frith's photographs of Great Britain for images of the towns, villages and streets where their ancestors lived; and, of course, photographs of the churches and chapels where their ancestors were christened, married and buried are an essential part of every genealogy tree and family album.

Frith Products

All Frith photographs are available Framed or just as Mounted Prints and Posters (size 23 x 16 inches). These may be ordered from the address below. From time to time other products - Address Books, Calendars, Table Mats, etc - are available.

The Internet

Already twenty thousand Frith photographs can be viewed and purchased on the internet through the Frith websites and a myriad of partner sites.

For more detailed information on Frith companies and products, look at these sites:

www.francisfrith.co.uk
www.francisfrith.com
(for North American visitors)

See the complete list of Frith Books at:

www.francisfrith.co.uk

This web site is regularly updated with the latest list of publications from the Frith Book Company. If you wish to buy books relating to another part of the country that your local bookshop does not stock, you may purchase on-line.

For further information, trade, or author enquiries please contact us at the address below:
The Francis Frith Collection, Frith's Barn, Teffont, Salisbury, Wiltshire, England SP3 5QP.
Tel: +44 (0)1722 716 376 Fax: +44 (0)1722 716 881 Email: sales@francisfrith.co.uk

See Frith books on the internet www.francisfrith.co.uk

TO RECEIVE YOUR FREE MOUNTED PRINT

Mounted Print
Overall size 14 x 11 inches

Cut out this Voucher and return it with your remittance for £1.95 to cover postage and handling, to UK addresses. For overseas addresses please include £4.00 post and handling. Choose any photograph included in this book. Your SEPIA print will be A4 in size, and mounted in a cream mount with burgundy rule line, overall size 14 x 11 inches.

Order additional Mounted Prints at HALF PRICE (only £7.49 each*)

If there are further pictures you would like to order, possibly as gifts for friends and family, purchase them at half price (no additional postage and handling required).

Have your Mounted Prints framed*

For an additional £14.95 per print you can have your chosen Mounted Print framed in an elegant polished wood and gilt moulding, overall size 16 x 13 inches (no additional postage and handling required).

> *** IMPORTANT!**
> These special prices are only available if ordered using the original voucher on this page (no copies permitted) and at the same time as your free Mounted Print, for delivery to the same address

Frith Collectors' Guild

From time to time we publish a magazine of news and stories about Frith photographs and further special offers of Frith products. If you would like 12 months FREE membership, please return this form.

Send completed forms to:
The Francis Frith Collection, Frith's Barn, Teffont, Salisbury, Wiltshire SP3 5QP

Voucher for FREE and Reduced Price Frith Prints

Picture no.	Page number	Qty	Mounted @ £7.49	Framed + £14.95	Total Cost
		1	**Free of charge***	£	£
			£7.49	£	£
			£7.49	£	£
			£7.49	£	£
			£7.49	£	£
			£7.49	£	£

Please allow 28 days for delivery	*** Post & handling**	**£1.95**
Book Title	**Total Order Cost**	**£**

Please do not photocopy this voucher. Only the original is valid, so please cut it out and return it to us.

I enclose a cheque / postal order for £ . . . . made payable to 'The Francis Frith Collection'
OR please debit my Mastercard / Visa / Switch / Amex card
(credit cards please on all overseas orders)

Number . . . .

Issue No (Switch only) . . . . Valid from (Amex/Switch) . . . .

Expires . . . . Signature . . . .

Name Mr/Mrs/Ms . . . .

Address . . . .

. . . .

. . . . Postcode . . . .

Daytime Tel No . . . . Valid to 31/12/02

The Francis Frith Collectors' Guild

Please enrol me as a member for 12 months free of charge.

Name Mr/Mrs/Ms . . . .

Address . . . .

. . . .

. . . . Postcode . . . .

Would you like to find out more about Francis Frith?

We have recently recruited some entertaining speakers who are happy to visit local groups, clubs and societies to give an illustrated talk documenting Frith's travels and photographs. If you are a member of such a group and are interested in hosting a presentation, we would love to hear from you.

Our speakers bring with them a small selection of our local town and county books, together with sample prints. They are happy to take orders. A small proportion of the order value is donated to the group who have hosted the presentation. The talks are therefore an excellent way of fundraising for small groups and societies.

Can you help us with information about any of the Frith photographs in this book?

We are gradually compiling an historical record for each of the photographs in the Frith archive. It is always fascinating to find out the names of the people shown in the pictures, as well as insights into the shops, buildings and other features depicted.

If you recognize anyone in the photographs in this book, or if you have information not already included in the author's caption, do let us know. We would love to hear from you, and will try to publish it in future books or articles.

Our production team

Frith books are produced by a small dedicated team at offices in the converted Grade II listed 18th-century barn at Teffont near Salisbury, illustrated above. Most have worked with the Frith Collection for many years. All have in common one quality: they have a passion for the Frith Collection. The team is constantly expanding, but currently includes:

Jason Buck, John Buck, Douglas Burns, Heather Crisp, Isobel Hall, Rob Hames, Hazel Heaton, Peter Horne, James Kinnear, Tina Leary, Hannah Marsh, Eliza Sackett, Terence Sackett, Sandra Sanger, Shelley Tolcher, Susanna Walker, Clive Wathen and Jenny Wathen.